ANTONI TÀPIES
NEW WORK

WADDINGTON GALLERIES 2010

ANTONI TÀPIES—RECENT PAINTINGS BY A GRAND MASTER

Looking at these very recent paintings of Antoni Tàpies, virtually all of which were completed in 2009, some thoughts spring to mind that maybe are worth pondering. Born in December 1923, he has of course, had a very long life in art and lived through a complicated historical epoch, all creatively spent in his beloved native Catalonia. He has throughout, always vigorously defended Catalonia's cultural traditions and over the course of more than sixty years significantly added to them. But he is in no way a simplistic nationalist. Equally he possesses the broadest culture always committed to what might be described as a fully Eurasian humanism and attitude to art, drawing on the eastern and western cultures of the greatest land mass of this planet, and on which originates so much of the art over thousands of years in which he and ourselves participate. From 1954, when he finally abandoned any pretence of possibly becoming a surrealist artist—rooted in a highly polished painterly representational language, in which he might easily have achieved great personal success—he has developed in each and every work, his own forms of concrete realism that bases itself in a tactile reality, in a language unlike any other, and that is entirely his own. There is a sense in which, for him, any material becomes like paint or crayon that he applies, or rather integrates, in each one of his works. Everything has the potential to become like paint, be it a book or a door, a chair or a basin. Paintbrushes become like paint itself; newspapers, concrete, the cast of a body part such as an arm, a footprint, a piece of red felt, the reverse of a stretcher, are all capable of transcending the art of collage and becoming part of a complex iconography as well as a tactile facture. There is a real sense in which Tàpies has found a way of transcending the collage art of artists such as Picasso and Schwitters, who of course, half a century earlier, made possible such forms of realism. Material becomes surface, and writing becomes gesture, always endowed with reflective, if usually elusive meaning, that deliberately avoids precise definition. Each and every one of his pieces sit beautifully within the tradition of the Spanish still life or *bodegón*, that stretches from Sánchez Cotán, who was active at the end of the Sixteenth Century, depicting his magnificent vegetables through to Zurbarán and Goya, and down to the great Picasso himself, who Tàpies met for the first time in 1951. (Already by 1948, he had met Joan Miró, also to become a huge influence, and a friend) These still lifes of the great Spanish masters are nearly always characterised by a dark monochromatic background that isolates the inanimate object. Objects are thus given a spatial infinity that highlights the uniqueness of each 'thing' whether magnificent cardoon, as depicted by Sánchez Cotán, to the severed heads of animals of Goya and Picasso. All these works of the Spanish tradition speak of different historical and personal realities that reflect the everyday, and yet peer into the strange mysteries of existence. It is no different with Tàpies, whose personal experience of the history of Spain and Catalonia in particular, in the traumatic central years of the Twentieth Century, define his art.

Yet success as an artist came early to Tàpies. In spite of the terrible repressions and cruelties of the Civil War, followed by the equally difficult years under Franco that Spain, and in a special way Catalonia, endured until 1975, he nonetheless quickly made an international career for himself. Even though as late as 1966 he spent a short spell in prison for having identified himself with the Catalonian Nationalist cause, yet he had achieved sufficient success by the very early 50s to have represented Spain in the Venice Biennale and other international exhibitions on both sides of the Atlantic. By 1953 he had already signed a contract with the legendary gallery of Martha Jackson in New York. Michel Tapié, the famous French critic, and friend of Francis Bacon, was a leading apologist in Paris at this time, and in England, Roland Penrose, the friend and supporter of Picasso and Miró, found in Tàpies the perfect representative of the continuity of the Spanish tradition. There is a sense though, in which this early success has been less than helpful to Tàpies' long-term fame in an era now overwhelmingly dominated by Pop and Conceptual art. Perhaps he is today seen too much as a grand survivor of a lost European period that included figures like Jean Dubuffet in France or Alberto Burri in Italy, who were part of a post-Second World War 'art brut' realism that is now art history, rather than of our time. This is not without a certain truth of course, but another more contemporary reading of Tàpies, as an artist, is possible. Art, as we have already implied, especially thinking of Tàpies, is full of potential ambiguities. Equally, one might read him as a prototype of the conceptual artist, who shares very precise affinities with Joseph Beuys. Beuys was born in 1921, only two years before Tàpies, and still today is a hero to so many young artists in a way that Tàpies is not, but surely deserves to be.

'Show your wound' is one of Beuys' most influential dictums. Certainly given the two archetypal traumas of mid-Twentieth Century European history – firstly the Spanish Civil War and then the Second World War, unleashed by German Fascism all over Europe, from the Pyrenees to the Urals, find in Tàpies and Beuys, generationally and through analogous imagery, an attempt to come to terms with a very specific historic past. Equally proposing through art a certain healing process, each artist uses the broken detritus of their own environments and cultures, to reconstruct and possibly mend, therapeutically, the destruction that took place all around them throughout their young adulthood. The cross is a central motif of many works of Tàpies and Beuys. For Tàpies himself, the cross may refer essentially to the mystical powers of addition, the 'plus sign'. But it is impossible for the cross not to evoke a Beuysian healing bandage, as well as, of course, the universal Christian symbol of salvation. Joseph Beuys projects himself essentially as a sculptor, Tàpies largely, though not exclusively, as a painter. There are of course other significant contrasts between the two. Tàpies, though he has written and made several statements on his own art and its broader functions, is an artist essentially of privacy and silence. Beuys on the contrary, particularly in the last two decades of his career, gave increasing prominence to the public and performing aspect of his creative process. However, in the sense that all creative processes are experiments, the results that both artists achieve have beautiful and surprising affinities for all the individuality of touch that each gives. Beuys similarly found strategies and routes to transcend the collage through the invention of what he described as 'social sculpture', whose meaning is in part left open to personal interpretation, through the engagement of the viewer. Perhaps one path into the works of Tàpies is to see them (using Beuysian language) as 'social painting'. In them, the material of the streets, whether it be a wall, a door, or a chair, a fragment of discarded clothing, the veritable earth or pavement on which we stand, have the ability to be transformed into art. The art that ultimately functions as a means of understanding and contemplation of the self and of the larger Universe, of which these fragments, often ruined and beaten up by historical circumstances and the ravages of time, are part.

Of course, all great art functions as a reflection on time, and acts as an aid to overcome our own sense of mortality. Tàpies has over many years developed his own strategies to make his particular syntax of marks, and his skills and knowledge are extensive and not borne lightly. His early work showed his consummate ability to make art as refined in its execution as the most detailed depictions of Salvador Dalí. Having such skills alone, gave him the power and authority to reject this path in favour of one more natural and unforced, even child-like (in a Paul Klee sense), and capable of drawing on traditions of east and west. Tàpies has acknowledged the influence of Zen philosophy and its visual representation through the work of the great calligraphers of China and Japan. But his work, unlike that of many Twentieth Century western artists who have fallen under the spell of the east, is never slavish imitation. The calligraphy that can be found in so many of his works is always his own, his playing with numbers and letters that allude to many traditions, Cabalistic, Christian and Muslim mysteries, as well as eastern philosophies, are nonetheless rooted in his own Catalan culture, and above all in his sense of self. Whether alluding to himself or to his beloved wife, Teresa, using the letter T that also stands for the cross and the healing plaster, his sense of gesture is always characteristic and never an imitation. Signs deriving from Cabalistic or Llullian numerical systems are at best, at least for most viewers, only half understandable. But this sense of half understanding is enough. The work of art is no treatise. We might know Ramon Llull as a Thirteenth Century Catalonian theologian, philosopher, mathematician, writer, and universal man but he is, of course, a national hero of his native land. He was the author of hundreds of volumes on every conceivable subject under the sun, including an imaginative novel ('Blanquerna', a love story), tomes on alchemy, law and religion. Tàpies has managed to amass a significant collection of incunabula and books by Llull, whose numerical systems, to which he often alludes in his paintings, are even claimed by some today as premonitions of modern computing systems. Be that as it may, one of his early major works is entitled 'Art Abreujada de trobar Veritat', that translates as 'The Abbreviated Way of Finding Truth'. Even as a title it is a beautiful way of describing each and every work by Tàpies, this most direct and plain speaking of artists. The art of memory also is at the core of Llullian philosophy, and equally lies at the very heart of Tàpies' lifetime project. For it is one thing for an artist to depict a landscape or a face, or a particular body. Tàpies, in his work, attempts and succeeds with something quite different. His art represents the aesthetic that always goes from the very particular to the general, from the descriptive to the philosophical and the political, always asking questions of the viewer. Only to look at one painting in this group of recent works, like 'Red knot' of 2009 (cat. no.7), might remind one of a beautiful assertion of Llull, who in his 'Book of Light' ('Liber De Lumine') asserts that 'this book is like a knot tied in a rope to prompt the memory to recollect things.' The artworks of Tàpies do the same, and encourage us to look at the entire world around us in his way, and through his eyes. The mystery of art, however, is that the artist has his or her unique way of presenting and perceiving the world and enlightening us with a particular perspective. To paraphrase Llull, only slightly from the preface to the same book, Tàpies' paintings are there in order to 'enlighten the intellect and stimulate it to understand intelligible things artificially and to discover natural beings with their secrets; this is meant to be an Art of Understanding subsidiary to the General Art from which it arises; and it deals above all with natural things associated to the intellect in providing doctrine about the light of truth. Its subject is that illumination with which all other sciences are illuminated.' Tàpies is, in his own way—to refer to Joseph Beuys once again—his own silent but highly significant 'Free University', in which he wishes us all to take part. He equally has contributed, in his very personal way, to a genuinely expanded language of art that is deserving of universal relevance now.

NORMAN ROSENTHAL
London, February 2010

9

ANTONI TÀPIES—PINTURAS RECIENTES DE UN GRAN MAESTRO

Al mirar las más recientes pinturas de Antoni Tàpies, casi todas virtualmente concluidas en 2009, vienen a la cabeza algunas ideas sobre las que valdría la pena reflexionar. Nacido en diciembre de 1923, ha tenido ciertamente una larga vida inmersa en el arte, vivida en una época histórica complicada, y realizada toda, desde el punto de vista creativo, en su amada Cataluña natal. Siempre, y sin cesar, ha defendido enérgicamente las tradiciones culturales de Cataluña, y a lo largo de más de 60 años ha contribuido a ellas de manera considerable, aunque Tàpies no adolece en modo alguno de un nacionalismo simplista. Al mismo tiempo, posee la más vasta cultura, siempre comprometido totalmente con lo que podría describirse como un humanismo euroasiático y una actitud hacia el arte que recurre a las culturas orientales y occidentales de la mayor superficie habitada del planeta, en la que se originó durante milenios la mayor parte del arte del que participamos tanto él como nosotros mismos. A partir de 1954, cuando Tàpies abandonó finalmente cualquier pretensión de convertirse en un artista surrealista, con un lenguaje representativo y pictórico de gran refinamiento—con el que podría haber conseguido fácilmente un gran éxito personal—ha desarrollado en todas y cada una de sus obras formas personales de un realismo concreto, basado en una realidad táctil, en un lenguaje sin parangón, que es, además, exclusivamente propio. Tiene un sentido, para él, en el hecho de que cualquier material se convierta en algo similar a los pigmentos o a los lápices que aplica, o mejor dicho, que integra, en cada una de sus obras. Todo tiene el potencial de convertirse en pintura, ya sea un libro o una puerta, una silla o un lavabo. Los pinceles son en realidad como la pintura misma. Periódicos, hormigón, el molde en escayola de una parte del cuerpo, como un brazo, una huella, un trozo de fieltro rojo o el revés de un bastidor, pueden todos trascender el arte del collage y entrar a formar parte de una compleja iconografía tanto como de una factura táctil. Hay un sentido real en el que Tàpies ha encontrado la forma de trascender el arte del collage de artistas como Picasso y Schwitters que, por supuesto, medio siglo antes hicieran posible esas formas de realismo. Cualquier material se transforma en superficie, y la escritura se convierte en gesto, siempre dotados de un significado meditado, aunque a menudo fugaz, que evita deliberadamente la definición precisa. Todas y cada una de sus obras se asientan admirablemente en la tradición de la naturaleza muerta, o bodegón, española, que se extiende desde Sánchez Cotán, a fines del siglo XVI, con sus magníficas hortalizas, a través de Zurbarán y Goya hasta el mismo gran Picasso, al que Tàpies conoció por primera vez en 1951. (Ya en 1948, había conocido ya a Joan Miró, que también sería para una enorme influencia, y un amigo). Estas naturalezas muertas de los grandes maestros españoles se caracterizan generalmente por su fondo oscuro, monocromático, que aísla al objeto inanimado. Los objetos adquieren así la infinidad espacial que acentúa la singularidad de cada "cosa", ya sea un magnífico cardo, como los pintados por Sánchez Cotán, o las sangrientas cabezas de cordero de Goya y Picasso. Todas estas obras de la tradición española hablan de diferentes realidades históricas y personales que reflejan lo cotidiano y al mismo tiempo se adentran en los extraños misterios de la existencia. No es diferente con Tàpies, cuya experiencia personal de la historia de España y de Cataluña en particular, en los traumáticos años centrales del siglo XX, define su arte.

Y sin embargo el éxito como artista le llegó pronto a Tàpies. A pesar de las terribles represiones y crueldades de la Guerra Civil, seguida de los años igualmente difíciles que hasta 1975 sufrió España bajo Franco, y de manera especial Cataluña, el artista se forjó rápidamente una carrera internacional. Aunque todavía, incluso tan tarde como en 1966, pasó una breve temporada en la cárcel por haberse identificado con la causa del nacionalismo catalanista, ya había conseguido suficiente éxito, a principios de los años 50, para haber representado a España en la Bienal de Venecia y en otras exposiciones internacionales a ambos lados del Atlántico. Para 1953 había firmado, por ejemplo, un contrato con la legendaria galería de Martha Jackson en Nueva York. Michel Tapié, el famoso crítico francés, y amigo de Francis Bacon, era en esos años uno de sus más destacados defensores en París, y en Inglaterra, Roland Penrose, amigo y admirador de Picasso y Miró, encontró en Tàpies al perfecto representante de la continuidad de la tradición española. Ese éxito temprano, sin embargo, parece no haber ayudado mucho que haya permanecido a largo plazo la fama de Tàpies, en un período dominado ahora en gran medida por el arte Pop y Conceptual. Es posible que hoy día se le considere sobre todo como el último gran superviviente de un período europeo perdido, que incluyó figuras como Jean Dubuffet en Francia o Alberto Burri en Italia, que formaron parte del realismo del 'art brut' posterior a la 2a Guerra Mundial, que es ya historia del arte y no historia de nuestro tiempo. Esto puede ser verdad, por supuesto, pero es posible también hacer una lectura de Tàpies, como artista, en clave contemporánea. El arte, como ya hemos dado a entender, especialmente cuando pensamos en Tàpies, está lleno de ambigüedades potenciales, que llevarían a interpretarle como prototipo del artista conceptual, como alguien que comparte afinidades muy concretas con Joseph Beuys. Este último nacido en 1921, sólo dos años antes que Tàpies, continúa siendo aún hoy día para tantos jóvenes artistas el héroe que Tàpies ya no es, pero que sin duda merece ser.

'Muestra tu herida' es una de las máximas más influyentes de Beuys. Dados los dos traumas arquetípicos de mediados del S.XX en la historia de Europa, en primer lugar la Guerra Civil Española y a continuación la 2a Guerra Mundial, desatada por el fascismo alemán en toda Europa, desde los Pirineos hasta los Urales, se puede encontrar ciertamente en Tàpies y en Beuys, cercanos tanto generacionalmente como por la analogía de sus imágenes, el intento de llegar a un acuerdo con un pasado histórico muy específico. Igualmente, al proponer través del arte un proceso curativo, ambos han usado los residuos rotos y desechados de su propio entorno y cultura para reconstruir, y posiblemente arreglar, terapéuticamente, la destrucción que tuvo lugar a su alrededor a lo largo de los años de su juventud. La cruz es un motivo central de muchas de las obras de Tàpies y de Beuys. Para Tàpies, la cruz puede referirse esencialmente a los poderes místicos de la suma o adición, del 'signo más'. Pero es imposible que la cruz no evoque al mismo tiempo al vendaje de Beuys, además de, por supuesto, el símbolo universal cristiano de salvación. Joseph Beuys se proyecta el mismo esencialmente como escultor, Tàpies, principalmente, aunque no en exclusiva, como pintor. Naturalmente, hay otros contrastes importantes entre los dos. Tàpies, aunque ha escrito y hecho declaraciones sobre su propio arte y sus funciones más amplias, esencialmente es un artista de la intimidad y el silencio. Beuys, al contrario, y en especial en las dos últimas décadas de su vida, dio cada vez más importancia al aspecto público y de *performance* de su proceso creativo. Sin embargo, en el sentido en que todos los procesos creativos son experimentos, los resultados que logran ambos artistas tienen afinidades especiales y sorprendentes, por toda la singularidad táctil que cada uno otorga a sus obras. Beuys encontró, de un modo parecido, estrategias y rutas para trascender el collage a través de la invención de lo que describió como 'escultura social', cuyo significado deja en parte abierto a la interpretación personal, a través de la implicación del espectador. Tal vez una trayectoria para introducirnos en las obras de Tàpies sea verlas (usando el lenguaje beuysiano) como 'pinturas sociales'. En ellas, el material encontrado en las calles, ya sea un muro, una puerta, un fragmento de ropa desechada, o un trozo del verdadero suelo o pavimento que pisamos, tienen la capacidad de ser transformado en arte. El arte que en última instancia funciona como el medio de comprender y contemplar el yo y la grandeza del universo, del cuál son parte también estos fragmentos, a menudo arruinados y golpeados por las circunstancias históricas y los estragos del tiempo.

Todo gran arte funciona, naturalmente, como una reflexión sobre el tiempo y ayuda a superar nuestro sentimiento de mortalidad. Tàpies ha ido desarrollando sus propias estrategias con el paso de los años para crear su personal sintaxis de signos, y sus habilidades y sus conocimientos son muy vastos y no pueden tomarse a la ligera. Sus obras tempranas demuestran una técnica consumada para crear un arte tan refinado en su ejecución como las obras más exquisitas y detallistas de Salvador Dalí. Sólo el tener esas soberbias aptitudes le dio poder y autoridad para rechazar ese camino en favor de uno más natural y menos forzado, incluso infantil (en el mismo sentido de Paul Klee), y capaz de recurrir, además, a tradiciones de Oriente y del mundo occidental. Tàpies ha reconocido la influencia de la filosofía Zen y su representación visual a través de las obras de los grandes calígrafos de China y Japón. Pero, a diferencia de muchos artistas occidentales del siglo XX, que han sucumbido al hechizo de Oriente, su obra nunca es mera imitación. La caligrafía que aparece en tantas de sus obras es siempre suya; por ejemplo, sus juegos con números y letras que aluden a muchas tradiciones, como los misterios de la Cábala, del Cristianismo y del Islam, sí como a filosofías orientales, están, sin embargo, arraigados en su propia cultura catalana y, ante todo, en su sentido del yo. Ya sea haciendo alusión a sí mismo o a su amada esposa, Teresa, usando la letra T, que también simboliza la cruz y el vendaje curativo, su sentido del gesto es siempre característico y nunca una imitación de otros. Los signos que derivan de los sistemas numéricos cabalísticos o de Ramón Llull son, en el mejor de los casos, por lo menos para la mayoría de los observadores, comprensibles sólo a medias. Pero este sentido de comprensión limitada es suficiente. La obra de arte no es un tratado. Podemos conocer a Ramon Llull como el teólogo, filósofo, matemático y escritor, y hombre universal, del siglo XIII, pero es también, naturalmente, el héroe nacional de su tierra natal. Fue autor de cientos de libros acerca de todo lo imaginable, incluyendo una imaginativa novela ('Blanquerna', una historia de amor), tratados de alquimia, derecho y religión. Tàpies se las ha arreglado para reunir una importante colección de incunables y libros de Llull, cuyos sistemas numéricos, a los que el artista suele hacer alusión en sus obras, son, según alegan algunos, premonición de los modernos sistemas informáticos. En cualquier caso, una de sus principales obras tempranas se titula 'Art abreujada de trobar veritat', (arte abreviado de encontrar verdad). Sólo ya como título es una atractiva manera de describir todas y cada una de las obras de Tàpies, el artista de habla más directa y sencilla. El arte de la memoria forma parte también de la esencia de la filosofía de Llull, y, del mismo modo, radica en el corazón mismo del proyecto vital de Tàpies. Una cosa es que un artista represente un paisaje o un rostro, o un cuerpo en particular. Tàpies, sin embargo, en su obra, intenta y logra algo totalmente distinto. Su arte representa la estética que va siempre de lo particular a lo general, de lo descriptivo a lo filosófico y a lo político, siempre haciéndole preguntas al espectador. Sólo mirar a uno de los cuadros de este grupo de sus obras más recientes, como 'Nudo rojo', de 2009 (nº7 del catálogo), podría recordarnos una admirable afirmación de Llull, que en su 'Libro de luz' (Liber de Lumine) afirma que 'este libro es como el nudo que se ha hecho en una cuerda para hacernos recordar algo.' Las obras de Tàpies hacen lo mismo, y nos animan a observar de ese mismo modo el mundo entero a nuestro alrededor, y a través de sus ojos. El misterio del arte, sin embargo, es que cada artista tiene su manera única e individual de percibir y presentar el mundo y de iluminarnos con su perspectiva propia. Para parafrasear a Llull, sólo brevemente, del prefacio del mismo libro, las pinturas de Tàpies existen para 'iluminar el intelecto y estimularlo a fin de comprender cosas inteligibles artificialmente, y descubrir seres naturales con sus secretos; esto tiene la intención de ser un Arte del Entendimiento secundario al Arte General del que proviene; y trata, ante todo, con las cosas naturales asociadas al intelecto proporcionando doctrina sobre la luz de la verdad. Su sujeto es la iluminación con la que se iluminan todas las ciencias.' Tàpies es, a su propia manera—para referirnos a Joseph Beuys de nuevo—su propia 'Universidad Libre', silenciosa, pero de gran importancia, en la que desea que todos participemos. Igualmente, ha contribuido, de su forma tan personal, a un lenguaje del arte realmente amplio, que merece ahora la aceptación universal.

NORMAN ROSENTHAL
Londres, febrero de 2010

1

Tres raspalls | *Three brushes*
2008
mixed media and collage on wood
$81\frac{7}{8} \times 67$ in / 208×170 cm

2

Franja blava | *Blue strip*
2008
paint, varnish and collage on wood
51¼ × 38⅛ in / 130 × 97 cm

3

Paisatge | *Landscape*
2009
paint on wood
63¾ × 51¼ in / 162 × 130 cm

4

Palangana | *Washbasin*
2009
mixed media and assemblage on canvas
63¾ × 51¼ in / 162 × 130 cm

5

Signes sobre marró | *Signs on brown*
2009
paint on wood
25½ × 32 in / 65 × 81 cm

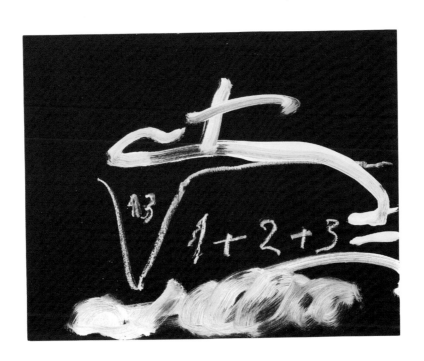

6

Ondulacions i braç | *Waves and arm*
2009
mixed media on wood
59 × 59 in / 150 × 150 cm

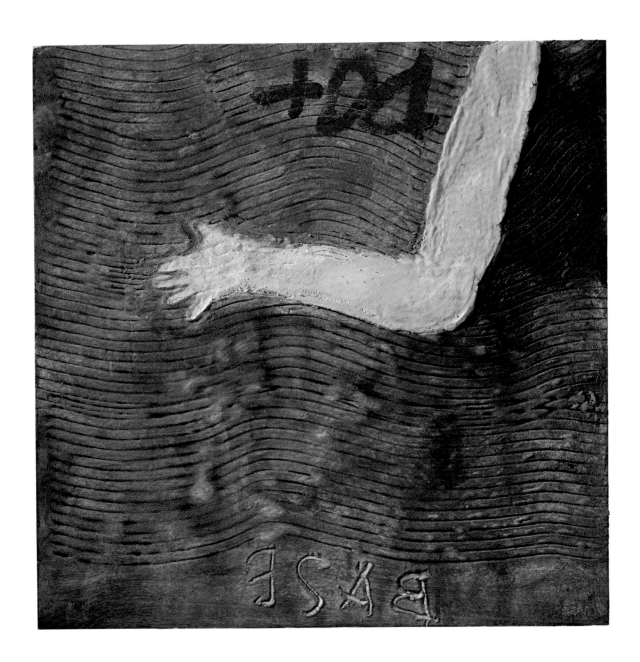

7

Nus vermell | Red knot
2009
paint and collage on wood
25¾ × 32 in / 65.3 × 81 cm

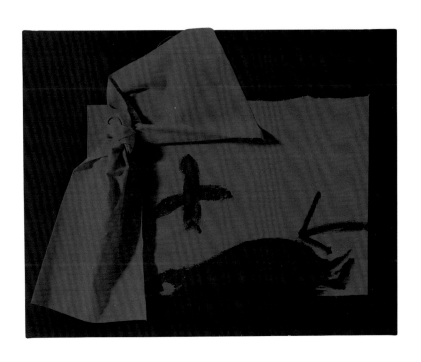

8

Escrits i formes sobre matèria | *Writings and forms on matter*
· 2009
mixed media on wood
106¼ × 86½ in / 270 × 220 cm

9

Signe d'amiració vermell | *Red exclamation mark*
2009
paint and ink on canvas
35⅛ × 45⅝ in / 89.3 × 116 cm

10

Protuberancies | *Protuberances*
2009
mixed media on wood
32 × 39⅜ in / 81 × 100 cm

11

Xifres vermelles | *Red figures*
2009
paint on wood
39¼ × 31⅞ in / 100 × 81 cm

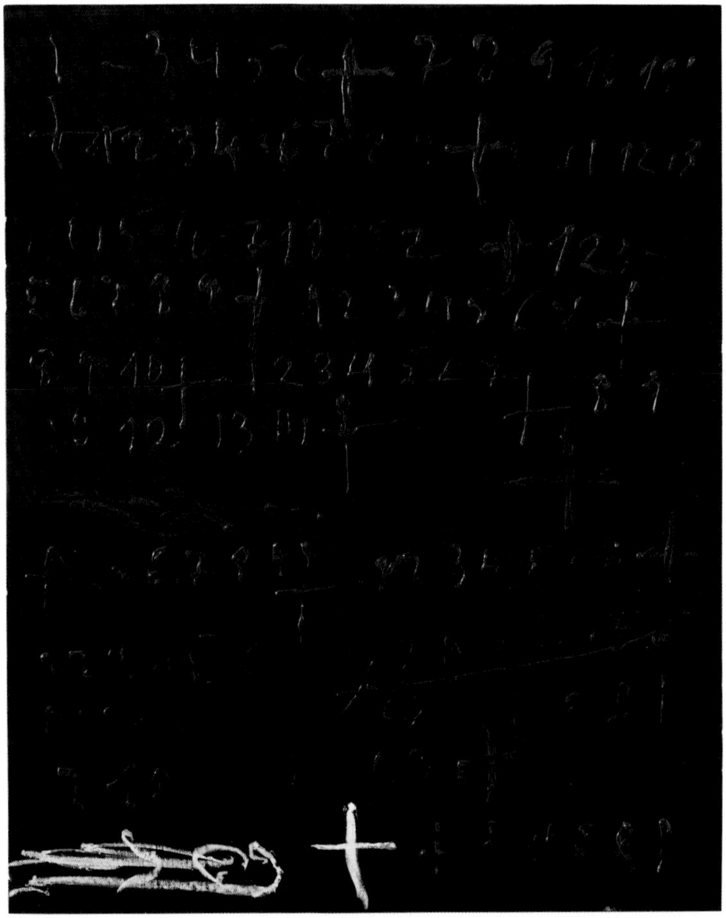

12

Matèria i diaris | *Matter and newspapers*
2009
mixed media and collage on wood
51⅛ × 76½ in / 130 × 194.5 cm

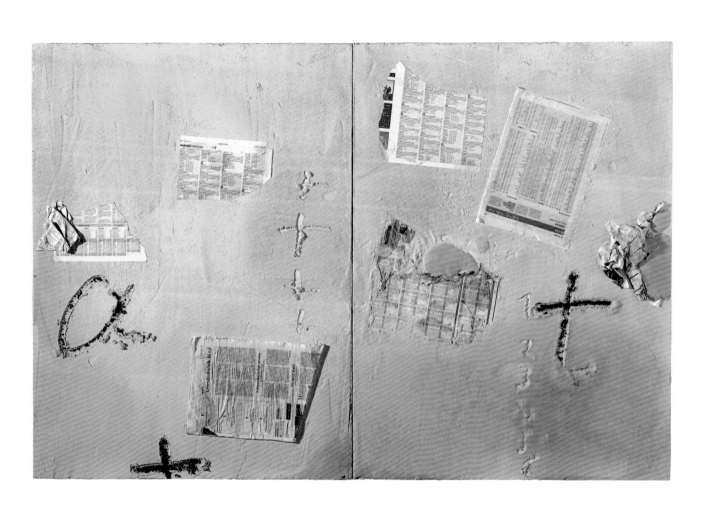

LIST OF WORKS

1
Tres raspalls | *Three brushes*
2008
mixed media and collage on wood
81⅞ × 67 in / 208 × 170 cm

2
Franja blava | *Blue strip*
2008
paint, varnish and collage on wood
51¼ × 38⅛ in / 130 × 97 cm

3
Paisatge | *Landscape*
2009
paint on wood
63¾ × 51¼ in / 162 × 130 cm

4
Palangana | *Washbasin*
2009
mixed media and assemblage on canvas
63¾ x 51¼ in / 162 x 130 cm

5
Signes sobre marró | *Signs on brown*
2009
paint on wood
25½ × 32 in / 65 × 81 cm

6
Ondulacions i braç | *Waves and arm*
2009
mixed media on wood
59 × 59 in / 150 × 150 cm

7
Nus vermell | *Red knot*
2009
paint and collage on wood
25¾ × 32 in / 65.3 × 81 cm

8
Escrits i formes sobre matèria | *Writings and forms on matter*
2009
mixed media on wood
106¼ × 86½ in / 270 × 220 cm

9
Signe d'amiració vermell | *Red exclamation mark*
2009
paint and ink on canvas
35⅛ × 45⅝ in / 89.3 × 116 cm

10
Protuberancies | *Protuberances*
2009
mixed media on wood
32 × 39⅜ in / 81 × 100 cm

11
Xifres vermelles | *Red figures*
2009
paint on wood
39¼ × 31⅞ in / 100 × 81 cm

12
Matèria i diaris | *Matter and newspapers*
2009
mixed media and collage on wood
51⅛ × 76½ in / 130 × 194.5 cm

All works have come directly from the artist

BIOGRAPHY

1923 Born in Barcelona, 13th December, into a liberal *catalanista* family

1926–32 His early education in Barcelona is disrupted by poor health and frequent changes of schools

1934 Begins his secondary education. The Christmas issue of the magazine *D'ací i d'allà* publishes a feature on the artistic avant-garde which makes a lasting impression on him. Teaches himself to draw and paint. Catalan autonomy is declared

1936 Outbreak of the Spanish Civil War

1940 Enrols in the Instituto Menéndez y Pelayo and later returns to one of his former schools, the Escuelas Pías, where he finishes his secondary education

1942 In the autumn, Tàpies develops a serious lung condition and enters the Puig d'Olena sanatorium in November. He stays there until June the following year reading extensively around German romanticism and Post-romanticism

1943 Convalesces in Puigcerdà, continuing to study literature and making charcoal and pencil sketches based on reproductions of works by Holbein, Pisanello and Ingres

1944–45 Briefly studies drawing at a school run by the painter Nolasc Valls but finds the teaching too academic. Begins a series of self-portrait drawings, a regular practice that continues until 1947. Begins his law studies at the University of Barcelona. Uses his sister's apartment on Carrer Diputació in Barcelona as a studio

1946 He continues working in this studio on Carrer Diputació where he creates his first non-figurative works, mostly collages made of string, thread, scrap paper and cloth. Mixes with a group of young artists exhibiting at the Club Els Blaus, Sarrià, and meets the writers J.V. Foix and Joan Brossa, as well as members of the group Els Vuit

1947 Meets Joan Prats, a prominent collector who introduces Tàpies to the work of Joan Miró. Continues to make collages while experimenting with *grattage* in his paintings. The cross, which will become a regular motif, makes its first appearance

1948 Visits Miró's studio with an introduction by Prats through whom he becomes increasingly interested in the art of Paul Klee. Cofounder of the avant-garde magazine *Dau al Set*, which publishes the majority of the texts in Catalan. Participates in the *I Saló d'Octubre* held at the Galeries Laietanes, Barcelona

1949 Participates in two important exhibitions: *Exposición antológica de arte contemporáneo*, Terrassa, and the *II Saló d'Octubre*, Barcelona. The poet João Cabral de Melo, the Brazilian consul in Barcelona, introduces Tàpies to Marxism

1950 Participates in the *VII Salón de los Once* at the Galería Biosca, Madrid which adopts a more radical line towards new art. Visits Salvador Dalí in Cadaqués. In October, obtains a grant from the French government to visit Paris where he hopes to find a gallery to show his work. The same month he holds his first solo exhibition at the Galeries Laietanes, Barcelona, which reflects his current interest in the work of the Surrealists. One of the paintings on show there is chosen for the *Pittsburgh International Exhibition of Contemporary Painting*. While living in Paris he begins *Història natural (Natural history)*, a series of nineteen pen and ink drawings completed the following year

1951 During his stay in Paris, visits Picasso at his studio in the rue des Grands-Augustins

1952 Represented by five works at the *XXVI Biennale di Venezia*. Shows a number of the works made in Paris at the Galeries Laietanes, his second solo exhibition. Participates again in the *Pittsburgh International Exhibition of Contemporary Painting*

1953 His first exhibition in the United States opens at the Marshall Field and Company Art Gallery, Chicago, but fails to find any buyers. Most of the works are shown again in October at the Martha Jackson Gallery, New York. During his visit he discovers the painting of the Abstract Expressionists in which he sees affinities with his own work

1954 Moves away from figurative imagery in order to focus on materials and texture. Begins working with latex, which gives his work greater density and monumentality. Makes another trip to Paris to try and establish contact with commercial galleries. Marries Teresa Barba

1955 Continuing his experiments with new materials, he begins to use a paste of varnish and marble dust impregnated with India ink and powdered pigments. Works on the theme of 'the wall' in which he explores the possibilities of painting as relief. Participates in a group exhibition *Phases de l'art contemporain*, organised by the poet and critic Édouard Jaguer. Takes part in the *III Bienal Hispanoamericana*, Barcelona, where he is awarded the Premio de la República de Colombia. Meets Michel Tapié, the author of the first monograph on his work, which is published the following year. With the help of Tapié he joins Rodolphe Stadler's gallery in Paris which opens in the autumn with a group show in which he participates

1956 His first solo exhibition in Paris opens at the Galerie Stadler in January. Included in *Recent Abstract Painting* at the Whitworth Art Gallery, Manchester, along with leading American and European painters. Works on his first large assemblage, *Porta metàl.lica i violí (Metal shutter and violin)*, a new direction he does not immediately pursue, although the twin themes of the shutter and door become integral to his work. Makes his first trip to Italy

1957 Organises an important exhibition of European and American abstract art, *Arte Otro*, at the Sala Gaspar, Barcelona, in which he brings together those artists Michel Tapié had grouped together around the idea of *art autre*: Appel, Burri, Dubuffet, Fautrier, de Kooning, Pollock, Tobey and Wols. Holds his first solo exhibition in Germany, at the Galerie Schmela, Dusseldorf

1958 Travels to Milan where his first solo exhibition in Italy opens at the Galleria dell'Ariete. Meets Lucio Fontana. Fifteen works are shown at the Spanish pavilion at the *XXIX Biennale di Venezia* in a selection of primarily abstract art. Awarded the Grand Jury Prize of the Carnegie Institute, Pittsburgh. Marcel Duchamp, one of the judges, becomes a firm supporter of Tàpies' work in the United States

1959 Following a successful solo exhibition at the Martha Jackson Gallery, New York, the Museum of Modern Art and the Solomon R. Guggenheim Museum each purchase a painting. Meets Robert Motherwell, Hans Hofmann and Franz Kline. Invited to show at *documenta*, Kassel. Cardboard becomes an important new element in his paintings

1960 Makes his first poster, on the occasion of the opening of the Museu d'Art Contemporani, Barcelona. In September, he participates in *New Forms-New Media*, a group exhibition with an international character held at the Martha Jackson Gallery

1962 In February, the first retrospective of Tàpies' work opens at the Kestner-Gesellschaft, Hannover, organised by Werner Schmalenbach. This is followed by a second retrospective in March, at the Solomon R. Guggenheim Museum, New York, organised by Thomas Messer. Tàpies spends the summer in his recently acquired farmhouse in Campins, a small village at the foothills of Montseny. In September, he works in St. Gallen on a mural for the library in the Handels-Hochschule

1963 Moves into a new house and studio in the Carrer Saragossa, Barcelona, designed by J.A. Coderch. The new space enables him to work on a larger scale

1964 In June exhibits eight large-format paintings at *documenta*, Kassel. At the beginning of November a large exhibition of works on paper from 1946 to 1964 opens at the Sala Gaspar, Barcelona. A major monograph by Joan Teixidor is published on the occasion of the exhibition

1965 In early June Tàpies visits London, where the Institute of Contemporary Arts is holding an exhibition of his work organised by Roland Penrose. During the summer he writes an important text on the influence of traditional painting on his own work, a text that he later publishes in an extended form as *La tradició i els seus enemics en l'art actual*

1966 In March, along with around four hundred students and a large group of intellectuals, Tàpies takes part in a clandestine assembly of the Democratic Students' Union of the University of Barcelona: all the participants are arrested. Five years later, Tàpies' participation is judged to be a serious misdemeanour and he receives a fine

1967 In November, attends the opening of his first solo exhibition at the Galerie Maeght, Paris, the start of a long relationship with the gallery with whom he has signed a contract. In addition to the exhibition catalogue, a special issue of *Derrière le miroir* is published with texts by Michel Tapié and Jacques Dupin

1968 In March, attends the opening of a retrospective at the Museum des 20. Jahrhunderts, Vienna, organised by Werner Hofmann, which travels to Hamburg and Cologne. Designs the stained-glass windows at the chapel of the Convent of Zion in Valais. Makes his first tapestry, for the *Tapestry Biennial*, Lausanne

1969 In February, a retrospective exhibition of his graphic work opened at the Kunstverein, Kassel, organised by Werner Schmalenbach, and with a catalogue introduction by Werner Hofmann. A film, *Antoni Tàpies* is produced by the Fondation Maeght, directed by Clovis Prevost

1970 Household objects such as plates, newspapers, clothes, brooms and baskets, as well as natural materials such as straw, play an increasingly important role in his paintings. A collection of the artist's writings, *La pràctica de l'art*, is published in Barcelona. Attends a clandestine assembly in the monastery of Montserrat, near Barcelona, to protest against the so-called 'Burgos Trial' in which a military court is judging opponents of the Franco Dictatorship

1971 Political themes find their way into his work, particularly in symbols of Catalan identity that also mark Tàpies' political resistance to the Franco regime

1972 Awarded the Rubens Prize in Siegen, Germany, which he receives at the opening of a retrospective at the Städtische Galerie in Haus Seel

1973–74 Tàpies is the subject of four retrospective exhibitions: at the Musée d'art moderne de la Ville de Paris; the Louisiana Museum of Modern Art, Humlebæk, Denmark; the Nationalgalerie, Berlin; and the Hayward Gallery, London, organised by the Arts Council of Great Britain. In May 1974, Tàpies publishes a second collection of his writings under the title *L'art contra l'estètica*

1976 A retrospective opens at the Fondation Maeght in Saint-Paul-de-Vence in July. This is followed in August by a retrospective at the Seibu Museum of Art, Tokyo. Designs a poster in support of a pro-democracy festival organised by the Congrés de Cultura Catalana and banned at the last moment by the authorities

1977 A retrospective opens at the Albright-Knox Art Gallery, Buffalo, New York and travels to Chicago, San Antonio, Des Moines and Montreal. An exhibition of works on paper from 1944 to 1976 opens at the Kunsthalle Bremen and travels to Baden-Baden and Winterthur

1978 The artist's autobiography, begun in 1966, is published under the title *Memòria personal: Fragments per a una autobiografia*. In the Spring, he attends the opening of an exhibition of his work at the Martha Jackson Gallery, New York, celebrating twenty-five years of collaboration between the artist and dealer

1979 Experiments with a new form of relief involving objects covered with material which has been sprayed with paint. Awarded the Premi Ciutat de Barcelona and is elected honorary member of the Berlin Academy of the Arts. A retrospective opens at the Badischer Kunstverein, Karlsruhe and travels to Kiel and Linz

1980 Tàpies is given his first retrospective in Spain, at the Museo Español de Arte Contemporáneo, Madrid, which includes more than two hundred and fifty works. In September, travels to Amsterdam for the opening of a retrospective at the Stedelijk Museum organised by Edy de Wilde

1981 Awarded the Medalla de Oro de Bellas Artes, Spain's highest honour in the fine arts. He is invested doctor honoris causa by the Royal College of Art, London. Creates his first ceramic sculptures with the German ceramist, Hans Spinner. Commissioned by the Barcelona City Council to design a monument to Pablo Picasso. A large assemblage of furniture and pieces of cloth contained within a crystal cube and a fountain is unveiled in 1983

1982 Publishes his third collection of writings under the title *La realitat com a art*. A retrospective opens at the Scuola di San Giovanni Evangelista, Venice, as part of the *XL Biennale di Venezia*. The Wolf Foundation of Jerusalem honour Chagall and Tàpies with their prize, the first artists to receive the award which previously had gone to scientists

1983 Completes a large mosaic for the Plaça de Catalunya in Sant Boi de Llobregat, Barcelona, with the assistance of Joan Gardy Artigas. Awarded the Gold Medal of the Generalitat de Catalunya. Honoured by the French government as an Officier de l'Ordre des Arts et des Lettres. Makes a number of freestanding ceramic sculptures of furniture, books, clothes and small objects with Hans Spinner at Artigas's studio in Gallifa. This collaboration continues over the next five years

1984 Awarded Rembrandt Prize by the Johann Wolfgang von Goethe Foundation, Basel. Receives the V Peace Prize from the United Nations Association in Spain. Constitutes the Fundació Antoni Tàpies in Barcelona

1985 Publishes a new collection of writings titled *Per un art modern I progressista*. Awarded the Prix National de Peinture by the French government, and elected a member of the Royal Academy of Fine Arts, Stockholm

1986 An anthological exhibition organised by Rudi Fuchs opens at the Wiener Künstlerhaus in Vienna, and travels to Eindhoven

1987 The city of Barcelona hands over the Casa Montaner i Simó, a Modernist building by Lluís Domènech i Montaner to the Fundació Antoni Tàpies. Tàpies shows his first bronze sculptures, casts of manipulated household objects, at the Galeria Carles Taché, Barcelona

1988 He is invested doctor honoris causa by the University of Barcelona. The Musée Cantini, Marseille, holds an exhibition selected from the artist's own collection of his work. Publication of *Tàpies. Obra completa 1943–1960*, first volume of the *catalogue raisonné* of the artist's work by Anna Agustí

1989 Appointed honorary member of the Wiener Künstlerhaus, Vienna. Elected honorary member of the Real Academia de Bellas Artes de San Fernando, Madrid. A retrospective opens at the Kunstsammlung Nordrhein-Westfalen, Dusseldorf, organised by Werner Schmalenbach

1990 Unveiling in February of the monumental aluminium and wire sculpture *Núvol i cadira (Cloud and chair)* made in collaboration with Pere Casanovas, on top of the headquarters of the Fundació Antoni Tàpies. Tàpies donates three hundred and eleven works to the Foundation

1991 Tàpies is commissioned to create a monumental sculpture for the new Museu Nacional d'Art de Catalunya: his projected sculpture of a giant sock causes considerable controversy

1992 Appointed honorary member of the Royal Academy of Arts, London, and of the American Academy of Arts and Sciences, Cambridge, Massachusetts. Creates a large mural for the Pabellón de Cataluña at the Exposición Universal, Seville, and a ceramic mural for the façade of the Musée de Céret, France

1993 Together with Cristina Iglesias, Tàpies is chosen to represent Spain at the XLV Biennale di Venezia and his installation Rinzen wins the Leone d'Oro. UNESCO awards him the Picasso medal

1994 A retrospective at the Galerie nationale du Jeu de Paume, Paris

1995 A major retrospective at the Solomon R. Guggenheim Museum, New York. Tàpies is made a foreign associate member of the Académie des Beaux-Arts de l'Institut de France, Paris. An exhibition of his graphic work is held at the Museo de la Casa de la Moneda, Madrid. The Catalan Government awards him the National Visual Arts Prize

1996 A major retrospective tours museums in Japan. Presented with the Cross of the Order of Santiago by the President of the Portuguese Republic in Lisbon

1997 Contributes to a forum on intolerance at the Académie Universelle des Cultures, Paris, with a paper titled 'Art between despotism and anarchy'. Retrospective at Museo Pecci, Prato. Presented with the Gold Medal by the University of Oporto. An exhibition of works from 1981 to 1997 opens at Kestner Gesellschaft, Hannover and travels to Krems, Austria

1998 An exhibition that spans over fifty years of his work on paper and cardboard is held at the Fundació Antoni Tàpies

1999 Tàpies' L'art i els seus llocs is published as well as a re-edition of Tàpies, a complete collection of Juan Eduardo Cirlot's articles and writings on the artist

2000 A retrospective at the Museo Nacional Centro de Arte Reina Sofía, Madrid. Takes part in the exhibition Encounters. New Art from Old at the National Gallery, London

2002 Receives the Premio Nacional de Grabado y Arte Gráfico awarded by the Calcografía Nacional and the Real Academia de Bellas Artes de San Fernando, Madrid

2003 Antoni Tàpies. Cos I llenguatge, organised by the Fundació Antoni Tàpies and the Diputació de Barcelona, begins a tour around different towns in Catalonia. The President of the French Republic appoints him to the rank of Commander in the Order of the Legion of Honour. Tàpies. Werke auf Papier 1943–2003 opens in the Kunsthalle in Emden, Germany

2004 The Museu d'Art Contemporani de Barcelona (MACBA) presents the exhibition Antoni Tàpies. Retrospectiva, for which the book Tàpies en perspectiva is published. The Fundación General of the Universidad Complutense de Madrid commissions him to design the poster for the summer courses of El Escorial. He attends the presentation of the documentary T de Tàpies, directed by Carolina Tubau and produced by Televisió de Catalunya. Antoni Tàpies. Una arquitectura de lo visible opens at the Fundación Marcelino Botín in Santander. In Madrid, Tàpies. Tierras opens at the Museo Nacional Centro de Arte Reina Sofía. He has other solo exhibitions in Barcelona at Galeria Toni Tàpies and in Rio de Janeiro at Centro Cultural Banco do Brasil

2005 San Sebastian and Barcelona present a joint work by Tàpies and José Saramago produced to support Elkarri, a social movement which advocates a model of peace and dialogue to resolve the Basque conflict. He attends a recital by the flamenco singer Manuel Cuevas to mark the tribute paid to him by the Festival Internacional del Cante de la Minas (La Unión, Murcia). A retrospective exhibition opens at the Hara Museum in Tokyo. Tàpies is awarded the Lissone Prize for his entire career. He produces the commemorative poster for the celebration of the 15th birthday of the Fundació Antoni Tàpies. Solo exhibitions open at Waddington Galleries in London and Galerie Lelong in Zurich

2006 The eighth volume of the artist's complete works is presented at a public event at the Barcelona Athenaeum in the middle of June. In November, three exhibitions of recent work open at Galerie Lelong (Paris), Galería Soledad Lorenzo (Madrid) and Galeria Toni Tàpies (Barcelona). At the same time, the exhibition Forms for the 21st Century. Recent Work by Antoni Tàpies, part of the Urban Majorities 1900–2005 Project, based at the Fundació Antoni Tàpies, opens at the IES Barri Besòs secondary school in Barcelona. A book entitled Le soleil vu de dos, with articles by Jacques Dupin and prints by Tàpies, is published. Towards the end of December, he attends the opening of the retrospective exhibition Tàpies' Posters and the Public Sphere at the Fundació Antoni Tàpies in Barcelona. Other solo shows of his work are mounted in Porto, Lisbon, London, New York and Toulon

2007 In June, an exhibition of paintings, prints and sculptures opens at EMMA-Espoo Museum of Modern Art in Espoo, Finland. Antoni Tàpies – Signs and Matter opens in August at the Museum Schloss Moyland, Bedburg-Hau, Germany. The exhibition Tàpies Posters and the Public Sphere, organised by the Fundació Antoni Tàpies, tours to the Cervantes Institute, Madrid, and to the Museu Valencià de la Il.lustració i de la Modernitat (MuVIM) in Valencia

2008 In February, two exhibitions – Galeria Toni Tàpies, Barcelona, and Waddington Galleries, London – present the artist's most recent work, produced in his studios in Barcelona and Campins during spring and summer 2007. The retrospective exhibition *Tàpies' Posters and the Public Sphere* tours to the Cervantes Institutes in Toulouse, Prague and Berlin. To mark the occasion of the artist's 85th birthday, D. Sam Abrams, Jordi Carrió, Marc Cuixart and Enric Satué edit the portfolio *Tàpies escriu (Tàpies writes)*, with a selection of texts by Antoni Tàpies and prints by Antoni Llena, Soledad Sevilla, Manel Esclusa, Pere Formiguera, Joan Fontcuberta and Eulàlia Valldosera. The portfolio is presented on 13th December at the Foment de les Arts i del Disseny (FAD), Barcelona

2009 Xavier Antich publishes the book on Antoni Tàpies, *En blanc i negre (1955–2003)*. Together with Indiana University Press, the Fundació Antoni Tàpies publishes *A Personal Memoir. Fragments for an Autobiography (Complete Writings. Volume I)*, the first English version of *Memòria personal. Fragment per a una autobiografia* (1977) by Antoni Tapies, and the first volume of the artist's complete written works. *Antoni Tàpies: The Resources of Rhetoric* opens at Dia Art Foundation, Beacon, New York in May. He participates in *Event*, presented by the Merce Cunningham Dance Company at the Mercat de les Flors, with five works from the Fundació Antoni Tàpies' collection. The exhibition *Antoni Tàpies: Materia e tempo* opens at the Museo MARCA in Catanzaro, Italy

2010 The Fundació Antoni Tàpies re-opens in March after two years of closure due to building renovation, with an inaugural exhibition titled *Antoni Tàpies. The Places of Art*

This biography has been compiled with assistance from the Fundació Antoni Tàpies and from two main sources:

Tàpies: The Complete Works, Vols 1–8, ed. Anna Agustí, Fundació, Antoni Tàpies Edicions Polígrafa, Barcelona, 1988 (Vol.1); 1990 (Vol.2); 1992 (Vol.3); 1996 (Vol.4); 1998 (Vol.5); 2000 (Vol.6); 2003 (Vol.7); 2005 (Vol.8)
Tàpies, Solomon R. Guggenheim Museum, New York, 1995

SELECTED PUBLIC COLLECTIONS

Albright-Knox Art Gallery, Buffalo, New York
Ars Nova Museum, Turku, Finland
Baltimore Museum of Art, Maryland
Carnegie Museum of Art, Pittsburgh
Centro Atlántico de Arte Moderno, Las Palmas
Centro Galego de Arte Contemporánea, Santiago de
    Compostela
Fondation Beyeler, Riehen, Switzerland
Fondation Maeght, Saint-Paul-de-Vence, France
FRAC Picardie, Amiens, France
FRAC Provence-Alpes-Côte d'Azur, Marseilles
Fundació Antoni Tàpies, Barcelona
Fundació Joan Miró, Barcelona
Galerie für Moderne Kunst, Hanover
Galleria d'Arte Moderna Ca' Pesaro, Venice
Galleria Comunale d'Arte Moderna, Bologna
Galleria Nazionale d'Arte Moderna, Rome
Göteborgs Konstmuseum, Göteborg, Sweden
Guggenheim Bilbao, Bilbao
Hamburger Kunsthalle, Hamburg
Hirshhorn Museum & Sculpture Garden, Smithsonian
    Institution,
Washington, D.C.
Instituto di Tella, Buenos Aires
IVAM Centre Julio Gonzalez, Valencia
Kiasma Museum of Contemporary Art, Helsinki
Kunsthaus Zürich
Kunstmuseum Basel
Kunstmuseum Köln
Kunstmuseum St. Gallen, Switzerland
Kunstmuseum Winterthur, Switzerland
Kunstsammlung Nordrhein-Westfalen, Düsseldorf
Louisiana Museum of Modern Art, Humblebæk, Denmark
Marion Koogler McNay Art Museum, San Antonio, Texas
Moderna Museet, Stockholm
Musée Cantini, Marseilles
Musée d'Art Contemporain, Montreal
Musée d'Art Moderne de la Ville de Paris
Musée des Beaux-Arts, Lyon
Musée national d'art moderne, Centre Georges Pompidou,
    Paris
Museo de Arte Contemporáneo de Caracas Sofía Imber,
    Caracas
Museo de Arte Contemporáneo Internacional Rufino Tamaya,
    México D.F.
Museo de Arte Abstracto, Cuenca, Spain
Museo de Arte Moderna de São Paulo
Museo de Bellas Artes, Bilbao
Museo Nacional, Bogota
Museo Nacional de Bellas Artes, Buenos Aires
Museo Nacional Centro de Arte Reina Sofía, Madrid
Museu d'Art Contemporani, Barcelona

Museu de Arte Moderna, São Paulo
Museu Nacional d'Art de Catalunya, Barcelona
Museum Boijmans Van Beuningen, Rotterdam
Museum des 20. Jahrhunderts, Vienna
Museum Bochum-Kunstsammlung, Bochum
Museum Folkwang, Essen
Museum Ludwig, Cologne
Museum Moderner Kunst Stiftung Ludwig, Vienna
Museum of Contemporary Art, Los Angeles
Museum of Fine Arts, Houston, Texas
Museum of Modern Art, New York
Museum of Modern Art, Shiga, Japan
National Gallery of Victoria, Melbourne
Nationalgalerie, Berlin
Reed College, Portland, Oregon
Saison Museum of Art, Karuizawa, Nagano, Japan
Sammlung Essl, Vienna
San Francisco Museum of Modern Art
Scottish National Gallery of Modern Art, Edinburgh
Seibu Museum of Art, Tokyo
Sintra Museu de Arte Moderna, Portugal - The Berardo
    Collection
Solomon R. Guggenheim Museum, New York
Sprengel Museum, Hanover
Staatsgalerie, Stuttgart
Städtische Galerie im Städelsches Kunstinstitut, Frankfurt am
    Main
Städtische Kunsthalle, Mannheim, Germany
Stedelijk Museum, Amsterdam
Sutai Pinacotheca, Osaka, Japan
Tate, London
Tehran Museum of Contemporary Art, Tehran
University Art Museum, University of California, Berkeley
University of Michigan Museum of Art, Ann Arbor, Michigan
Van Abbemuseum, Eindhoven, The Netherlands
Washington University Gallery of Art, St Louis, Missouri
Wilhelm Lehmbruck Museum, Duisburg
Williams College Museum of Art, Williamstown, Massachusetts

Waddington Galleries would like to thank
Sir Norman Rosenthal for his introduction
to this catalogue

ANTONI TÀPIES NEW WORK
21 April–15 May 2010

Waddington Galleries
11 Cork Street
London
W1S 3LT

Telephone + 44 20 7851 2200
Facsimile + 44 20 7734 4146

mail@waddington-galleries.com
www.waddington-galleries.com

Monday to Friday 10am–6pm
Saturday 10am–1.30pm

Photography by Gasull Fotografía, Barcelona

Designed by www.hoopdesign.co.uk
Printed by www.fandg.co.uk

Published by Waddington Galleries
Co-ordinated by Louise Shorr

ISBN-978-0-9558285-8-4

p.1: *Franja blava* | *Blue Strip*, 2008, paint, varnish and collage on wood, 51¼ × 38⅛ in / 130 × 97 cm (detail, cat. no.2)